I0881116

COINING A WISHING TOWER

COINING A WISHING TOWER

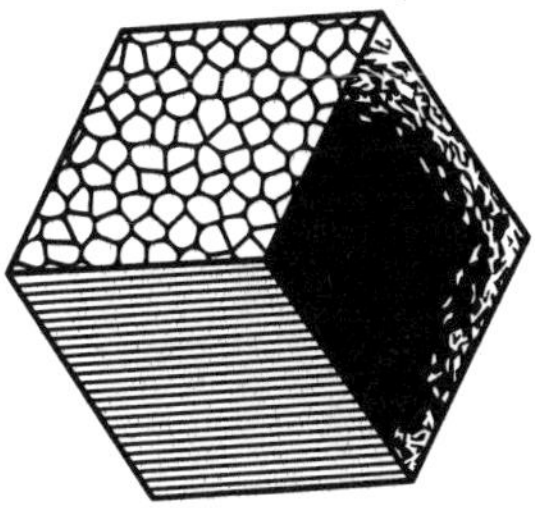

AYESHA RAEES

RADIX
BK CO-OP NY

All words copyright © 2024 by Ayesha Raees
All rights reserved.

ISBN 979-8-9894902-1-9

Editor
Meher Manda

Interior Layout and Design
Lantz Arroyo

Jacket Design
Nicholas Hurd

Printed and published in Brooklyn, New York by Radix.

Radix Printing & Publishing Cooperative
522 Bergen Street
Brooklyn, New York 11217

radix.coop

Praise for *Coining a Wishing Tower*

"Ayesha Raees's *Coining a Wishing Tower* is everything I hope to find when I read a book of poetry—fearless reckoning with unprecedented experience spoken in a singular, deeply and importantly strange lyric voice. My luck, to get to help introduce it to you. Your luck, to get to read it for the first time."

—Kaveh Akbar, *Martyr!*

"You are entering a world of Ayesha Raees' making, a lyric fable woven in tight silk strands. Singular in its voice and imagination, *Coining a Wishing Tower* is unyielding in its search for truth, for a spiritual tether. Its allegories remind us of what's holy in the everyday: a mother's faith, a father's machinery, a moon in love with a goldfish, the omniscience of Google. She writes, 'On fifth avenue, I want to be important. I want to hammer a nail into the New York sky. I want to hang myself on its wound' That's Raees daring you to leave unchanged."

—Ruth Awad, *Outside the Joy*

"Ayesha Raees' *Coining a Wishing Tower* is a beautiful epic, told through prose poems that surprise with precise and wondrous language. Raees thinks through art, place, family, life, and the afterlife, animating the collection through various characters—House Mouse, Godfish, the moon—and mediating it all through a Pakistani, Muslim, and woman speaker, who traverses racialized and gendered spaces' pilgrimages of faith and of the imagination; knowing and unknowing. In this debut, we find a bright and wild new voice in poetry."

—Cathy Linh Che, *Split*

"With *Coining a Wishing Tower*, Ayesha Raees' intercultural, interreligious meditation on family life, childhood, memory, and death, comes a bold imagination populated with a cat and a moon both in love with a Godfish, a House Mouse who performs rituals, where death is one such ritual, and a child who tells their father that 'The bare minimum to life...is to just live.' At its core, this collection wrestles with grief amidst life between cultures, religions, and geographic places. After hammering a nail into the sky, the speaker reveals, 'I want to hang myself on its wound,' and so too, was I rapt, hanging on the words of Raees' fashioned wound."

—Diana Khoi Nguyen, *Root Fractures*

"Ayesha Raees's *Coining a Wishing Tower* is an exciting debut collection that traverses multiple dimensions and landscapes, both metaphorical and physical. By skillfully playing with the theme of real or not-real, Raees invites the reader to meditate on what constitutes 'real' in the first place. The poet explores multiple other themes that play off one another—longing, belonging, departure, arrival, life, death, prayer, performance, and love, to name a few—through recurring figures that reflect and refract one another's desires. By rendering the figures' thoughts and situations into prose poetry, Raees also formally illustrates the various enclosures that serve to both trap and liberate the figures. Smart and imaginative, *Coining a Wishing Tower* is one worth reading over and over for the rich imagery and storytelling; a book that offers a new discovery at each savoring."

—Emily Yoon, *Find Me as the Creature I Am*

For Ghosts
Fractured Lands
Parental Shade

Indeed, to we belong and to we shall return

1.

House Mouse was running to the mountains but nothing came out of its climbs. Every peak held another peak, and every reach held another reach. At the end of all possible height, House Mouse found itself inside a tower. The tower looked like a black, elongated box, sharp at the edges, smooth and silky on the sides.

Behind all there was was just was: a view called beautiful only because it was now distant.

2.

My mother enjoys the healthiest bamboo broom. It cost her fifteen rupees and only five calories were lost in the Battle of Bargain. I am not in her army but she drags me into the field. The enemy's armor is poor, has a big gnawing hole right around where his heart should be. I do not believe ten rupees more or less could change him or his life. Above me, the sun turns my country to a boil. I clear my throat. I start my training for bargains. I say to him, *Hello, As-salamu Alaikum*. My mother hits me with the broom.

3.

The moon waxes only for one goldfish named Godfish. Godfish lives in the crystal clear aquarium behind the crystal clear window of a giant wooden house in New London, Connecticut. Burdened with monotony, Godfish entices the moon. It stripteases by floating upside down at night. Once the cat noticed this—believing Godfish had died—ruptured the night with its cry.

4.

Pakistan is the worst country in the world, but I am at the MOMA, staring at a Picasso. I hate my dirty shoes. My mother is very far, but I can still hear her every cough. On fifth avenue, I want to be important. I want to hammer a nail into the New York City sky. I want to hang myself on its wound.

5.

House Mouse is dancing in the tower. The tower is an archaic tower with one window shaped as a slit in the roof. It is a glassless breathless crack of a sunroof through which House Mouse cannot even see the sun full. Silence is not an option for the night. Crickets are cricketing and owls are hooting. There are fireflies on the ceiling and they are blinking. House Mouse has no language to describe this kind of disco.

6.

The body is a temple but only of a woman for a man who knows no prayer. My mother grew up in a foliage where an empty tree had nothing to do with a season. In her own crossings, the travel mustered a distance longer, embracing long stretches of a desert made up of golden sand. My mother once begged the sky for water and the land for grain.

7.

New London is a small, white town in Connecticut. Wikipedia says, in 2010, it held 26,984 individuals. Pakistan has a population of 197 million individuals. Saudi Arabia holds 32.94 million individuals. America, including New London, Connecticut, in 2018, is home to 327.2 million individuals. I have never been to New London, Connecticut, but I had my first Starbucks in Makkah.

8.

On the phone, my father says he is stuck. An important hand has disappeared from his mind. He needs it to build himself a machine. The machine, he mumbles and grumbles, is a coaster that would bring him to a tower where he can finally find his dislocation. The machine is his answer to my every question. The machine is my father's made-up thing.

9.

The cat has been in love with Godfish since the day the cat set its eyes on Godfish. Godfish, with all its heart, believes in only two things: love and being eaten by the cat. The cat spends most of its day checking out Godfish. The cat loves the way it shimmers against the sunlight. The cat loves the way it plays upside down in the moonlight. The cat only leaves Godfish's side to shit.

10.

House Mouse cooked fish for the first meal, corn for the second meal, and melted cheese for the third meal. The tower is one room full of great imaginings working towards not staying imagined. The tower's job is to provide, to turn every fantasy into a concrete actuality. The tower is a wishing tower. A wish a coin. But House Mouse is a simple being without much want. House Mouse was once like the tower itself—all House Mouse used to do was fulfill. House Mouse wishes to save the tower from its conditioning. House Mouse begins to perform rituals and chants in wish.

11.

On the phone, I tell my father my true ally would take care of my mother. My father parks the car at the side of Canal Bank Road and weeps into his palms. The Lahore Canal swells in the summer and dies in the winter. It carries the water to where the grain grows. The machine he wants is a fantasy to aid escape. The best machine is the brain. *The bare minimum to life*, I coo at him, *is to just live.*

12.

Google says New London, Connecticut, has four colleges. One for all levels of class and interests. I googled the weather in December and it can get pretty cold. I don't know how cold. It's not the best place to sleep outside. Or live outside. Or be outside. Google says New London, Connecticut, is not a small town but a small city. Thank God.

13.

When I entered Makkah, I was fifteen and on my period. We had all come to pray, to perform a lesser non-obligatory pilgrimage, but I couldn't. My mother said I was dirty. When I stopped bleeding, we took a cab to a mosque named Masjid-e-Ayesha, a place where women arrived to bathe themselves clean for the pilgrimage. It was the last week of Ramadan in August, and the next day I was to keep my first fast. The water of the shower held the desert's warmth. It held reminiscence of my mother's past. But the air I breathed was a new place. It was a place I needed to clean myself for.

14.

The moon has no choice but to wax or wane. The moon is not an independent thing. The moon relies heavily on the sun to be seen. On its own, the moon can only rise the water or sink it. The moon is in love with Godfish. The moon wishes to one day be able to rise Godfish and its waters to its lips.

15.

House Mouse knows of many rituals, but the one that gives liberation is through the number twenty-three. House Mouse cleans the tower twenty-three times, boils the water twenty-three times, steeps the tea leaves twenty-three times, and drinks it in the moonlight twenty-three times. After twenty-three days, House Mouse puts its face against the tower's walls and feels its rocks lose heat. Go cold.

16.

The giant wooden house in New London, Connecticut, was populated by one human, one cat, and Godfish. The human was the least important presence in the house for it was seldom there. The wooden house rested in the middle of a robust forest and was centric to many windings, convolutions, and unnatural happenings. What connected the wooden house to the real life giant black road was a Desire Path.

17.

The other name for Masjid-e-Ayesha is Masjid-e-Taneem. Google says Taneem means *to be blessed or to be given blessings*. Google says Ayesha means woman or life. My mother says it was the name of the Prophet's most beloved and youngest wife, the one who led an army at the battle of Jamel, and, therefore, has no real meaning unless meaning is given to it. I am named to embrace a woman famed for her rebel. I am named to embrace an existence that has no independent meaning.

18.

Godfish believes the way the sun warms up the aquarium is intentional. It isn't. It is an inevitable thing, a consequence of light, the nature of the sun being the sun. Yet, blinded, Godfish swims robustly during the day to devour, swallow, and inhale the sun. Godfish feels like the centerpiece in a joyfully disturbed snow globe where the liquid is liquid-glass nurturing in itself a friendly fire. Godfish feels it is a future conserved in a rejuvenating crystal ball.

19.

Something happened along the way to somewhere and that something gave birth to a feeling of resignation that either takes over or shrinks to the tiniest thing without entirely vanishing. My father, in his dream, has been asked to duty. My father wakes to a new year with one rotting leg, his car split in two on the new year road, with his eyes milking away a forever bruise. My father in an accident is just an incident we talk over on the phone. He chuckles at the dent he emitted on our planet. He no longer speaks of flying or machines.

20.

To practice shame is part of the education. Close the legs otherwise Satan will climb between them. Cover the head otherwise Satan will take a piss on it. Hide the breasts otherwise Satan will convince the body every single breath the lungs take is full of seduction. In Masjid-e-Ayesha, I emerged washed and clean in a fresh abaya and everyone said, *MashAllah*.

21.

The tower's rock was no longer churning. House Mouse feared its wish for liberation meant the tower was dead. House Mouse punched the walls and received nothing back, not even a cracked bone. The crickets and the owls muted. The fireflies fused. The silence seeped so deep into the night it turned mercilessly to give in to the day without a bird's call. Through the roof's slit, the sun did its job well, beaming so strong House Mouse felt a mock. The tower's final wish-fulfill was a wish that resulted in its own kill.

21.5

My mother says, *Without our faith, we are just a hollowing hallowing carcass.*

22.

A Desire Path is created through an inevitable erosion by an animal. It is a constant back and forth trod in the same narrow area. It is a natural act that connects two suffering destinations in their lack of constant hold. No one liked coming to the giant wooden house in New London, Connecticut, where the winter had a bad bite, the summer brought strange pesticides, and spring hardly lasted in the rain. There was no path, no trod, and no desire deep enough for any kind of create.

23.

My mother covered my eyes and guided me towards the big black box. *The first time you see the Ka'bah*, my mother whispered, filling my ear with an excitement rare for her disposition, *any wish you wish will come true.* To orchestrate a desire from a heart is impossible, for I had practiced my wish of the first sighting to a degree my desire had turned dull and tired. Yet, when the hands moved away from my eyes, I began my performance. In front of the towering box, sharp at the edges, smooth and silky on the sides, decorated with gold Arabic, I performed my prayer. I widened my eyes. I gaped my lips. I cupped my hands. I muttered and coined my wish. My mother reminded me to blow it out after my Ameen. This way it will reach the heavens faster.

24.

The sun is an inevitable thing. A body of no real self. A star so full of duty it has burnt its own conscience, its own soul, its own exist. For Godfish to fall in love with a big yellow bright inevitable thing was, to Godfish, nothing but fate. Godfish believed the sun only warmed Godfish, was only attentive to Godfish, and left Godfish every night only to inevitably return to its side every morning. Godfish believed the morning twilight held the sun's robust blush for Godfish and its evening twilight its shameful remorse for having to leave Godfish. One dawn, Godfish wished, with great heart, to go on a journey, for the air to become so thick with vapor, it would become an ocean. It would allow a big possible swim, up and up towards the sun.

25.

House Mouse cooked nothing for the first meal, nothing for the second meal, and nothing for the third meal. There was a concave in House Mouse's chest that rested on its bones. House Mouse was breathing its last few breaths. In the hunger, sickness was born, and House Mouse was full of images that danced without allowing the body much sleep. In this forever dream state, House Mouse was escaping from the tower, scurrying down from every top, undoing every zealous reach, and climbing back into the security of the past where House Mouse was just a normal mouse in a normal house. House Mouse wished there was no new horizon that ever greeted its door, that its dreams were held where dreams should be held– away from reality. But the tower was dead, and House Mouse wasn't just yet. The wishes were now just a consequence of choice and suffering.

26.

Google says cats learn by observation. In New London, Connecticut, there was only one cat in the big wooden house who felt more and more whole every passing day. In observation of Godfish, the cat's heartbeat raced with an intensity of nine cat hearts. The cat's body turned and rolled with Godfish's turn and roll. During the day, the cat glided and ran around the room, finding spots of sunlight on the floor to lie in, moved only when Godfish moved. Love is mimicry. Mimicry is mockery. Godfish detested the cat as much as the cat loved Godfish. Godfish's detest showed with an act of balanced apathy and reject.

27.

In Medinah, what my mother calls prayer, I call wish. My mother never asked me what I wished for when I first saw the Ka'bah. My mother never told me what she wished for when she first saw the Ka'bah. Every shadow held her wistfulness, a sigh that held a forever yearning. Her body heaved without a self, and my father was found always in linger two steps behind, a forever anticipation that resulted only in more wait. In the hotel room, I slept with my mother on the queen bed, my brother on the couch, and my father, without question, on the mattress on the floor. I told my mother the wish I wished to the big black towering box. My mother grasped her tasbeeh, washed me with nothing but a glassy, unblinking stare. I felt around me a surge of water, held together in collect, in duty, by a bulletproof glass so thick even my father's snores failed to penetrate it. I watched my mother mutter Ameen, blow it at me, and drown as soon as I grew gills.

27.5

Mama, I wish to leave.

28.

The winter solstice gave the moon its longest wax but not its fullest. The moon, mistaking long for best, began to plot and plan. To prepare a home, the moon emptied one of its best craters and tucked it away from the surface to a deep beneath where the sunlight could, even in its full fervor and heat, never reach. The moon filled the crater with water and used its pulsating core to keep the water warm. This is where Godfish will live, close to the moon's center, tucked away from any harm, any sight.

29.

During the ritual of death, House Mouse realized that, just like in sleep, there was no concept of time or space, and anything could lead to anything, alarming, charming, or calming, and it would be treated as nothing but a normal thing. The ritual revolved around House Mouse breathing out five times, saying thank you five times, saying sorry five times, praying for a brighter day five times, cursing the cold tower for its betray five times, and forgiving itself for all the hurt it had inflicted on both self and other five times. The last exhale of the lung took place when the day was in an in-between. In this twilight, the sky dripped red from a tear between light and the absence of it.

30.

At the airport, my mother cried. My father didn't. All hands rested heavy on my head. My bags held unfitted sheets, a paraat, and an oversized winter jacket my father had bought for himself that one time he went to Japan during a December. When I sat on the plane, my mother called me to convey her astonishment of how I did not cry even one single time, how my face, in her eyes, shone like a rural sky. When the wheels lifted and the phone slowly tore itself away from a land that was so used to being left, my body became an enveloping escapable closure of containment where the air was made of breath, where the limbs had as much potential to lift as to rest. I tried to converse with the mother next to me but she pulled her child away.

31.

Following are the things House Mouse heard after its death: *Have you ever seen the rain return to the sky? Every drop of water you have touched has once been to the sky. Have you ever been to the sky? It's a top place but there's still a topper place than the sky. Would you like to go higher from here? There is no way for the sky to take back the rain in ways we can see. So we must trust it. Do you have it in you? Trust? The earth is too strong, and the sky is, in the end, just a halfway in-between two somewheres. It is just a passage. But don't worry, the rain becomes rain even if we can't see it. What goes up comes down. Returns. You must learn to trust it. Transcend it.*

32.

The greatest country in the world is America. You don't even have to ask Google. Google will tell you on its own. All you have to type in the search bar is Greatest. Come on. Go. Try it. Like this, we can all know the world at our fingertips. The great children of America have eaten, at least once, McDonald's, which, to me, is relatable because I, too, as a child, in Pakistan, have eaten McDonald's, and have owned a collection of toys from the Happy Meal, which I displayed proudly on a toy shelf, which is still placed in my room in Lahore, behind protective glass, at home. These toys are different from the toys American children get. I believe. I believe. I believe.

33.

I was in seventh grade when my grandmother passed away. It was August, and my mother, father, and I, drove down from Lahore to Bahawalpur, a palace city built by the golden sand of the Cholistan Desert, where everyone was gathering for, as my mother put it, One Last Time. My brother stayed behind for an important exam he couldn't truly miss so, in my argument, who was there and who was not there, became so transparent it was concrete. Upon arrival: explicit tears. My Nani was lying on the charpai, cleaned and wrapped in cotton cloth, her wrinkles unmoving. Was she smiling a peaceful smile? Or did we want her smile to be a peaceful smile? Her Mona Lisa moment, I called it and everyone looked at my mother in utter dismay.

34.

The Ka'bah is a black box, sharp at the edges, smooth and silky on the sides, with gold verses calligraphed on each face. Or that is what its skin is. The cloth that covers the building hides the building. It separates the audience from what is behind. Is it a truth no one thinks of? Has no allowance for? The default has become to trust, and in this blind faith, all small gods are squeezed together to become one singular Big God. The cloth is a veil that hides the carcass, decorates it in a sleek beauty, allows for majesty. The Ka'bah is Allah's home, a home Muslims travel towards only to revolve around it, coining at it, in verses, prayers, desires, for cleanse and fulfill.

35.

It doesn't matter how they lived, when they die, they all say the same thing; *May they be granted a place in Jannat-ul-Firdous.* Back when I was a child but not considered much of a child, I couldn't pronounce Jannat-ul-Firdous until my mother sat me down and mouthed it to me, asking me to follow her lips. A word cannot be learned if there is no meaning unless it is a name calling so concrete it becomes both name and meaning, becomes an unquestioning identity. *Who is Firdous*? I asked, making my mother laugh and laugh, her eyes slanting, her neck bulging. *A place,* she breathed out, *a place in heaven that is of the highest level, reserved for the most pious, the most special, the most loved. If Allah deems it to be.*

36.

The moon has no sense of time but contains, in its nature, both virtues of patience and impatience. To have order is an obedience which comes in bondage with the sun. *What am I*, the moon laments in its revolves, *if not just a reflection of another louder being*? Yet, to possess desire is both an ailment and an aliment, to love not a condition but an experience. It is to take place between two bodies in either momentary infatuation or an elongated familiarity occurring in togetherness. The moon, in its effect and cause, becomes a lively thing, in love with Godfish swimming in the waters of an aquarium sea, without a sense of real time.

37.

When I Google it, there are many different results. Some say that Islamic heaven has one thousand levels, each as far from each other as the stars from our eyes, seeable yet unreachable. Other results say, there are only seven heavens, and they are after the stars in the big dipper or the planets in the solar system. Google says the word for seven in the Quran should not be taken literally for it can mean *several* and, therefore, *many*. All in all, our placement in all these heavens is determined by how much good we do. Each level has its own level of comfort, love, and privilege. Can we surpass this level and enter the next? Google says: *We won't ever feel the need to.* Inside us, all such desires, envy, and yearnings would be removed. Any kind of remembrance of our past lives, any regret, every love: it will all be erased.

38.

When I was a child but not much considered a child, my mother said that on the day of judgement, no one would care about the other, no parent for their child, no friend for their friend, no lover for their lover. *Will you forget me too*? I asked her. *It's inevitable*, my mother replied, *you will forget me too.*

39.

My father parks the car outside of the pizzeria where my friends have collected themselves with balloons, gifts, and cheer. I am turning nineteen. Inside the car, the August heat gathers itself in beads of sweat on both of our foreheads, a commonality of our genes where when we sweat, we sweat from our scalps. My father rests his hand on my head. My father pats. He never fixes the AC in his car. My hair is full of heat; I wonder if I can set his hand on fire. My father wishes me happy birthday. My father launches into lament soaked in advice. My father traps me. The car seat becomes a wooden platform, the seat belt a hammer, and my hand a trigger that sets off the spring. I was a catch, a pest, a rodent, a mouse, famed to always know how to help itself while still desiring an exit. I was a House Mouse dreaming of running away to a place full of height.

40.

Google says: *No! Cats have one life just like any other living creature! The fiction of feline immortality is due to how cats function! In awed resilience! Prone to survival! Yet in a fashion that is always barely!* To survive and heal and continue, cats strive in chapters, skipping from one existence to the other, from birth to separation to shelter to settlement to abandonment to ravagement to wilderness to car accidents and then to eventual demise. Each chapter becoming a disappearing act from the last, a knowing deeply settled in a body, a knowledge that permanence is a human fantasy, that in the end, living is dying many times in one singular life, to grow and adapt is a technique to survive, to give adherence to a lineage is continued as a mark that we were all once here, occurring in the narratives of the ones that will lead us into the future.

41.

The body is a vessel. The soul its context. House Mouse was surprised. It had died. Yet, it was alive. The conscious was halved, balancing in either too much clarity or too much blur. There was convolution. But also a linear path. It was like existing in all three states at once. House Mouse realized that death was again a journey. Can it be called life itself? House Mouse dipped in and out of memory. From one scene to the other. In one scene, House Mouse scurried outside a door to enter a corridor with no other door. When House Mouse started to run, the walls started to run as well, leaving House Mouse behind. In this scene, House Mouse was in a field so lush it looked as green as if on the other side. In front of House Mouse was a house House Mouse had once left for height. This was subconscious, House Mouse realized, its gaze getting larger and larger as the house itself grew larger and larger, feeding on all the distance House Mouse had once climbed.

42.

Google says there is something called a Barzakh. When someone dies—like a mother, a father, a friend, a lover—the body goes into the earth, and the soul enters an in-between, a period of wait, a journey that is determined by how good or bad one has been and therefore is. After death, two angels come to the soul for a quiz, and if the soul does well, gets a good grade, the angels will accumulate a GPA to the very ninth of a decimal which will determine the soul's next place of exist. The soul gets to be in either an in-between that is heavenly, *Illyin*, or hellish, like the core of the earth, *Sijjin*. Every quiz and grade determines a journey so special it is one-of-a-kind. Google says Islamic Barzakh is like Christian Limbo

43.

House Mouse left behind its body. The tower left behind its concrete. What was left was time and occurring. Suns and storming. Disintegrations. Erosions. Quakes. One evening, the tower, in rot, toppled. All that height once sought after turned into a dirt pile with a carcass inside. Now on the ground, every generation called it a burial site until it was no longer a sight but a mark on the land, disappearing gradually.

44.

My mother grinds her teeth in her sleep, and my father talks to himself in full wake. My mother locks her bedroom door, shuts down the ceiling fan, and naps. My father sits on the couch and says, Ama *Ama Haaii Ama*. My mother was born after thirteen years from a second marriage. My father an orphan boy full of guesswork. My mother watches *Eat Pray Love*. My father Facebooks. When they spend time together, they spend it collecting debris to assemble some kind of rock. They try to recall and remember. They sit in each and every room of a very big house with walls full of picture frames and clocks. Outside every window, the sun is so strong, it lights up every floating particle of the once invisible dust.

45.

It is December and the giant wooden house in New London, Connecticut, piles up in snow. The walls of the house burn in heat. The radiators bang, echoing throughout the house's empty. The cat yowls in discomfort. The cat pants pants. The water in the aquarium gets hot. Godfish's blood gets warm. There is stress in Godfish's swim. There is anguish. The windows perspire, drips drip. What is a wooden house if not a countdown to a fire? The wooden house pants pants, exhaling and inhaling heat, with a big risk of rupture. The wooden house cannot handle, cannot allow this smother. The wooden house cracks open a window, the one near the heating aquarium in the room full of cat yowls and torment. Immediately, the pants cool to a breath, the muscles relax, everyone de-stresses. Outside, constant snow. Whiteness in fall. Outside, a full moon, waxing aloud, eyeing down.

46.

Google says Barzakh is an Arabic word which means *obstacle* *hindrance* *separation* or *barrier*

47.

Google says Limbo is defined as (*in some Christian beliefs*) *the supposed abode of the souls of unbaptized infants, and of the Just who died before Christ's coming* or as *an uncertain period of awaiting a decision or resolution; an intermediate state or condition* or as *a dance*

48.

I call my mother every Sunday. In between our Sundays, I call her every when-I-can. We occur without fixed patterns, and I find my mother always awake. Always available. The more time I spend away from her, the more I call her. The more I call her, the more she becomes available. Over the phone, I mouth explain to her. Justify to her. Lament to her. *If you slit me*, I say, *you will find rubble and debris but never any rock.* I*f you slit me, you will find all the houses in all the cities where we began our lives only to end without ever finishing them. If you slit me, you will find so much split, you will be overwhelmed.* My mother, instead of watching me, has listened to me grow old. Grow ill. Grow lone. She lies in bed at 4AM. I lie in bed at 6PM. We are in twilight. In the forever in-between. In moments of chronic transit. *Why would I*, my mother asks, *slit you*?

49.

The moon is not human. The moon is a routine. The moon is a pouncer. The moon is a chance seeker. The moon only knows what is given to it. The moon does not wait for the winter solstice. The moon does not wait for its full wax. The moon looks at the open window the wooden house has opened, and mistakes the wooden house to be its friend, its ally, its shot. The moon throws its light through the opened window, through the glass of the aquarium, through the water to touch Godfish. Godfish looks up and finds the silver to hold no real heat, no real warmth. It is just a white cold alien spotlight. Godfish begins to run.

50.

Once upon a time I was in middle school, I wore uniforms, bought parathas for lunch, and studied good. My father woke me for school, made me breakfast, and was my driver, my carer, my machine. During morning car rides to school, my father did not allow opened novels, last minute homework, or tunes. This was the only time my father could talk the kind of talk other spaces stifled him out of, other spaces where his say, he believed, did not exclusively belong to his own. The living room held the television. The dining table meals. My mother and my brother loud and about. Every normal requiring performance. Every normal gave him only exhaust. But the car which held us together, held us in the comfort of transitions, was a place where things said and unsaid could be said and unsaid. In the car, my father became my father.

51.

With every mustered strength, the moon lifts the water, rounds Godfish into a dripping ball and pulls it through the opened window only to bring it to a float and a hover in the storming snow of New London, Connecticut. In the howling wind, Godfish squirms, and the water ball drips and spills. But the cold comes as a rescue, the freeze begins to create skin, to hold the water in, to stop the drip, and to grant the moon the continuation to blindly string.

52.

Get along, my father tells me at the airport before my first flight. *Get along with everyone despite everyone*, my father tells me in the overheating car. *Get along despite their gods, their skins, their thoughts*, my father tells me sobbing by the canal, his voice shaking on the phone. *Get along despite the difference and the indifference*, my father tells me as he packs my school lunch. *Get along like a machine that is less human, less right, less wrong.* My father, jobless again, zones out in front of the politicians barking at each other on the TV screen. *Get along even if it's too quiet, too full of anticipation, too full of potential.* My father runs a comb through my hair and braids it with blue and white ribbons. I am just eight, and I have an asthmatic chest that rattles all night, and everyone begs me to *please don't die, to please breathe fine*. EQ over IQ, my father types on the Facebook chat as America thunders against my bones, gives birth to throat lumps and ill-brained thoughts. *No more fights. Just nod and smile. And do what I could not do*—my father's voice disappears from my hearing as the phone goes into static—*get along.*

53.

The moon eventually realized. The moon should have waited for its best wax, just before its worst wane, to take advantage of its full face. For through its full face, the moon would have held the sun's strongest gaze, and be able to pull and pull without any potential of fail. The mistake was being blinded with chance. The mistake was not realizing winter would ice the water down. The mistake was to believe that a chance was only called a chance for it could never occur again. As the moon failed in December, as the snow of New London, Connecticut, gathered, the moon gave in. The moon drops the half ice, half water crystal ball back towards earth. Even in its best disposition, the moon realized it was still not the sun.

53.5

On the side of the unlit highway, a gold smeared fate—lost.

54.

It gets cold in New London, Connecticut. I don't want to Google how cold. I am always too scared to. The cat is yowling, jumping out of the wooden house's window and running through the snow, staring as the water becomes crystal, becomes solid, becomes heavy with potential to a quick fall. The cat wishes to give Godfish a rescue. The cat wishes to return Godfish back to its aquarium home. Inside the crystal ball, Godfish's orange swirl creates a pattern of potential deduce, of a future predict, but the ball grows heavy, and the moon is a shameful weak thing full of wordy zeal with no limb no bone no real substance to match its hungered soul. The moon loses its lift of the water body. The moon is not strong enough to support Godfish in its heavy, to give power and aid to its climb. On the side of the road, far away from the cat's cushioning crouch, the crystal ball crashes, its newly formed skin rupturing away to shatter and slush, the patterned future losing its future without ever fulfilling its shot at predict.

54.5

Mama, slit me and find inside me: predict.

55.

When the cat finds Godfish, it is no longer Godfish but just a fish. Fish is lying in a collection of cracked bones and bloodied flesh, a squash of browning, reddening scales, a mouth smashed closed. Against the stark white snow, against the black tar of the road, a spot of orange, red, and gold, once full of life, now just an estranged mark on the road. The night flushed into twilight. The sky ruptured. No more snow, just the sun coming out with winter heat, its gleam full of severe equality, normalcy, passive apathy. The cat feels its heart, once as full as possessing nine hearts, turn into a singular drown, an anchor which falls on and on for a bed rest that can only now rest once the heart rests. When the soul transcends from one exist to the next, will the cat see Godfish after its own death? Or will death cleanse the cat so truly it will not even remember Godfish? Would death tear them apart to a degree of absolute forget? For now, the cat lives and Godfish lives somewhere inside it. For now, the cat coils around the fish's body and refuses to leave its side until its side becomes absolutely obsolete. Until everything becomes absolutely obsolete.

56.

There was a house. A wall divided a garden in two. The gate held a latch always unlatched. Inside: a car. Inside: a door. Inside: a couch. On the couch sat a body of age staring at a ticking clock. The ticking clock does the wait ing wait ing
wait ing tock. There is a picture frame. There is no picture. There is no dust. The couch is covered in a white cotton cloth. The TV is on. The TV is gone. There is also another body of age. Then there is not. The house is so bright. The sun is so hot. The temperature is so high. The house is empty. The clock is gone. There is no body. There is so much dust. House Mouse is here. House Mouse has returned.

Acknowledgments

To my best friend, sister, and soulmate, Quynh Huong Vo, whose passing allowed me to seek the question of height, and to try my best to understand love, death and afterlife through this book.

To my best friend, brother, and queer fighter, Anique Ashraf who passed on when crossing Route 23 in New London, Connecticut. You make me think of the beyond while allowing me to fight for a present where you might have existed.

To my mother, father, Aanish Bhai, Sarah, and Zozo for a love that paralyzes me. Your support goes beyond the definition of my own rubric of mattering. Your support means I have worth in just being.

To Asian American Writers' Workshop and Kundiman for seeing me for the first time and strengthening my voice to join a community advocating for Asians and Asian American existences and stories. For making me realize that my body is also a body of matter and being. Thank you: Jyothi Natarajan, Emily Jungmin Yoon, Hala Alyan, Cathy Linh Che, Kyle Lucia Wu, Yasmin Majeed, Pik-Shuen Fung, Jen Lue, Zena Agha, t. tran le, and Huiying B. Chan.

To Kaveh Akbar for first seeing this book. To Platypus Press for bringing it first into being.

To Radix for an afterlife, a resurrection fitting the very themes of this book. I am grateful for Lantz Arroyo, Nicholas Hurd, and Meher Manda.

I am beyond grateful for all those who have reviewed and read this book. Thank you to Kaveh Akbar, Cathy Linh Che, Emily Jungmin Yoon, Diana Khoi Nguyen, and Ruth Awad for your incredible blurbs.

To friends. All of them.

To New York City for belonging, joy, and community. To Lahore for being a solace, an anchor, a root. To a place of great marking, Bennington College. To a place of another death and afterlife, University of Miami.

To my immigration lawyer, Emily Wages, for your support, mentorship, and care.

To this book for holding me together in my shatter. To giving allowance to be in a world bigger than my own world. For giving me liberation to stay and leave and stay and leave. However much I like to.

Thank You.

Ayesha Raees is a poet and artist identifying as a hybrid creating hybrid poetry through hybrid forms. Her work strongly revolves around issues of belonging and dislocation, G/god and spirituality, and beauty::cruelty while possessing a strong agency for decolonial, anti-violence, and anti-erasure practices. She edits poetry at *The Margins* and has been endorsed by the Asian American Writers' Workshop, Kundiman, UNESCO, and others. Her first book, *Coining a Wishing Tower*, won the Broken River Prize and was published by Radix in 2024. She is based in New York City and Lahore, Pakistan (and many other unsettled spaces).

About the Publisher

RADIX is a worker-owned, union printer and publisher based in Brooklyn, New York. We publish fresh perspectives, prioritizing the voices of typically marginalized communities. Our name comes from the Latin root of the word *radical*, meaning to get to the root.

Our books have won awards from *Foreword Reviews* and AIGA.

Colophon

At Radix, we pride ourselves in owning the means of production, and in crafting books that will give the reader joy from the moment the book is in their hands.

We printed this book on 70# Mohawk Via Vellum text stock with union labor in Brooklyn, New York, using an AB Dick 9995 offset press.

The cover was letterpress printed in gold foil on 100# cover stock, using a Heidelberg Windmill, a press that exudes timelessness and quality.

Other Radix Titles

The Land is Holy
noam keim

We Are Many: Defending Women & Sex Worker Human Rights
Anthology, ed. Beldan Sezen & Adam Shapiro

Is This How You Eat a Watermelon?
Zein El-Amine

Mortals
John Dermot Woods & Matt L.

Fanning the Flames: A Molly Crabapple Coloring Book
Molly Crabapple

There Is Still Singing in the Afterlife
JinJin Xiu

BINT
Ghinwa Jawhari

We Are All Things
Elliott Colla & Ganzeer

Futures: A Science Fiction Series
Various

Aftermath: Explorations of Loss & Grief
Anthology, ed. Radix Media